Reflective Communication Scrum /

Recipe for accountability

Betteke van Ruler

First printing october 2014
ISBN 978-94-6236-461-5
ISBN 978-94-6274-194-2 (E-book)
NUR 810

Published, sold and distributed by:
Eleven International Publishing
P.O. Box 85576
2508 CG The Hague
The Netherlands
Tel.: +31 70 33 070 33
Fax: +31 70 33 070 30
e-mail: sales@budh.nl
☛ www.elevenpub.com

Concept and text
Betteke van Ruler

Graphic design
Bianca Spierenburg | Studio Polkadot

Project management and translation
Frank Jansen | Desire to Communicate

Photography
Gidion Peters | Scrum Company

Photography Betteke van Ruler by
Jaap van der Klomp and Sjaak Ramakers

Copyright © 2014 Betteke van Ruler

Reflective Communication Scrum

/ This is how you do it

- The RCS Building blocks described
- What does the process look like
- Sprint and scrum, all in good time

2

/ Betteke van Ruler's **Reflective Communication Scrum**

Professional accountability

vision
1.
- on the profession
- on priorities

Decisional & Social accountability

intake
2.
- Assignment
- Ambition
- Team
- Project backlog

sprint planning
3.
- Goal & strategy
- Sprint backlog
- Alliances
- To do list

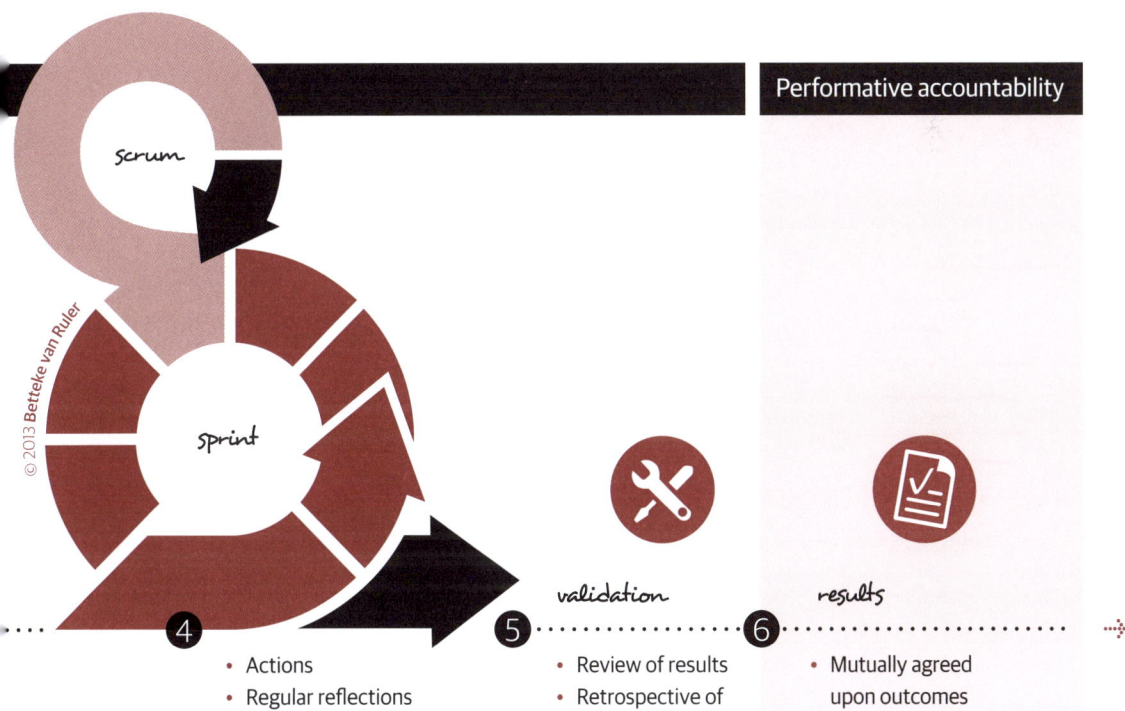

/ **Basic principles of the RCS**

/ Planning of interventions in timeboxed sprints
/ Reflecting (daily scrum) in short intervals during the sprint
/ After each sprint, validation of sprint and ambition
/ The team is collectively responsible for each step
/ The Scrum master facilitates the team during the process
/ The project owner participates in the process
/ Co-creation with key stakeholders for best results
/ Actions must be easy to adjust

Tight in method, flexible in content

/ **Key elements of the Reflective Communication Scrum**

4 Roles
Project owner
Scrum master
Development team
Project stakeholders

4 Meetings
Intake
Sprint planning
Daily scrum
Sprint validation

4 Artefacts
Project story
Project backlog
Sprint backlog
Showable results

☛ See **Chapter 3** for elaboration of the key elements of the RCS

/ Building block 1a: **Vision on the profession**

What is the added value of the communication branche and to whom? Opinions on this question differ substantially, but unfortunately the question is rarely discussed in public.

Visions classified
For one person, a communication professional should provide support to the implementation of company policy by ensuring a positive attitude or behavior of target audiences. For another, his or her value lies in establishing the connection between the organization and what is considered important in society. Again, for others, the key task of the communication department is to focus on developing the communicative qualities of the staff. Coaching and training of employees is then viewed as its most important contribution. In most textbooks it's either one or the other. To me, these different visions are not mutually exclusive: all belong clearly to the territory of any corporate communication or public relations department. Not as visions, but as strategies.

The reflective function

To survive and thrive, an organization above all requires credibility from (parts of) society. The only way to achieve that is to connect with what society finds legitimate. That calls first of all for monitoring and understanding what issues people are talking about and in what way. This is often called strategic counseling of management, and I see this as a reflective function of corporate communication or public relations: a continuous reflection on what society experiences as legitimate and the organizations' response to that. Especially today, when confidence in organizations is at an unprecedented low, I would suggest that this is a core function of the profession.

The four Cs of the branche

I believe that the field of corporate communication and public relations can be defined by four Cs. The C of counseling is the reflective function and the core of the profession. By applying that function the communication professional puts the 'style of the house' on the map: how do we interact with each other, how do we approach the outside world, and is this how we want it to be. All actions by organizational members are communicative, they all show something to others. That is why this counseling function is ultimately about the behaviors of all people in the organization, and consequently about their norms and values. The C of coaching is about helping employees to behave according to the chosen 'style of the house'. The C of conceptualization is about developing appropriate programs in the style of the house. For that you need a good methodology, for example the Reflective Communication Scrum. The last C is about creation, the development of fine interventions that match with the preferred style of the house and will be helpful to meet the organization's ambitions. That is all about tactics.

/ Building block 1b: **Vision on priorities**

Communication professionals often complain that they are overloaded with work. So you need to set priorities. But how or what?

Successful department
Not much research has been done on what makes a team or corporate communication or public relations department successful. Teachers often think it's all about proper training, and to scholars it is often about using the correct theory. Heads of departments tend to think that it is the size of their department that will make a difference. Professionals are convinced they will be more successful when appointed to be an advisor. One thing becomes clear from the scant research: all the above does not make the difference.

Better policy
The key is a good match between the CEO or the C floor person responsible for the communication portfolio, and a team that understands all about their priorities.

The art lies in being able to speak the management lingo, but especially in understanding what the management needs truly are. 'Focusing on the business', as a noted advisor at GKSV, Frank Körver, calls it. In the public sector it's called 'focusing on policymakers'. Not by timidly executing their ideas and directions, but by assisting them in doing the right things and do these in the right way.

Match
From an older study on how the most reputable companies in Europe have set up their communication, it appeared that the match with the corporate culture is of crucial importance. When the organization relied heavily on protocols, so did the corporate communication or public relations department. Where creativity and entrepreneurship predominated, that was also the guideline for the communication team. Linking up with the management culture was apparent. If management focuses on 'agile', then it may be important to start working with agile methods, too.

Choosing priorities
Choosing priorities means looking at the mission of the organization, understanding the probability of complications the organization might encounter and knowing which direction the organization has set out for itself, but not necessarily to obediently do anything the management or the board requires you to do. The emphasis of course is mainly on contributing to the realization of the strategic choices. But sometimes this means that space must be reserved for internal discussion in order to arrive at management decisions that will be better understood by the stakeholders of the organization, and are therefore likely to be more readily accepted. This calls for an intelligent mix of service and wisdom; and last but not least, for knowing your own toolkit, suitable theories, methods and tactics. That is how you can find your professional priorities.

/ Building block 2: **Intake**

Someone in the organization approaches the communication team with a request, or the communication team itself signals communication shortcomings either within or outside the organization. What to do?

Clear assignment

Communication professionals are often tempted to 'get on with the job' without a clear brief. With the RCS method such an assignment is considered an essential start. Most of all because along with the assignment there is a person who wants something done. In Scrum this person is essential. He or she is the person who 'owns' the project, as it were. He or she or a delegate is called the project owner and is by definition committed to the project and accountable as such. However in quite a number of instances the assignments are vague in nature, like: 'write me a brochure', or 'we need more communication'. That is why the first task of the team is to narrow the assignment into a shared ambition and shared project story.

First analyses

Sometimes some analyses are needed to create a shared ambition. Not, as in the old communication plan, in order to form a smart objective, but only to identify what the client should really want. To do that properly the professionalism of the team is of the utmost importance. The Scrum master facilitates the team to question the usefulness of ideas, propositions and decisions of the client. The team considers tightening up the wording of specific elements, or may want to know answers to questions like: 'why is it so necessary to produce a website? And why just now? What do you really want?'

Communication professionals usually start by analyzing the pros and cons of the matter: what does the problem really look like? That is done in the RCS too, by the team and the project owner, facilitated by the Scrum master. Analyze who are to be considered stakeholders of the project, and what their interests are. I also call for analysis of what people really think of the topic, the so-called 'social stories', just to identify what kind of further analyses should be considered as items in the project backlog.

Adjustment of the assignment

Based on the initial considerations the case will become much clearer, and you can then modify it accordingly. Sometimes further research is required, for example when you need to know more about the background and underlying (political) notions, or about what happened when this or a similar case was at hand in earlier days. Or you may want to have contact with stakeholders before commencing the project in order to involve them and get their commitment. Chances are that all this leads to revision of the job, or maybe even its cancellation. Sometimes this happens later, in the first sprint.

/ Building block 2: **Intake**

Ambition

Without ambition you will get nowhere. The intake phase should result in the definition of the ambition of the project: what is it the client wants as an outcome? Is your organization reorganizing and is this project a first part of it? Are citizens to be influenced to change their behavior in a particular way? Is the ambition to get people to develop sympathy for your proposition, product or service? Does the organization need to improve its image or goodwill? Try to formulate an ambition as a storyline, a narrative of the work, e.g. 'for such and such reasons we want to achieve this and that and we have to take care of x and y'. This helps you to focus, set priorities and share the story of the project with whoever is to be involved. The ambition of the project relates above all to the results.

Final team

In the intake you must decide which persons qualify for cooperation in achieving the ambitions. You must accept that communication on its own is not a powerful enough tool to solve every problem. Very often qualities and competencies are required which can only be found in other departments in the organization. Scrum prefers to work with multi-disciplinary teams. Anything goes, as long as it helps to achieve the ambitions of the project.

Project backlog

It is in this phase that we brainstorm and determine which ideas and actions are to be put on the preliminary repertoire list of actions, the so-called project backlog. In IT they call these actions 'user stories'. After that is done, it is preferable to define what has priority and what comes later, and design an initial portfolio of the project.

Lastly it is necessary to decide how long the sprints will take and when the daily scrums can be planned.

/ Building block 3: **Sprint planning**

When the intake is complete, planning of the first sprint can begin. As the Scrum method is fairly new to the communication field, and with lack of much experience we are not 100% sure of what sprint planning should comprise. It also depends on the situation and options, but I suggest at least the following.

Sprint goal and strategy
First, you must determine what you want to achieve in this period. Of course, the goal of the sprint needs to build up into achieving the ambition of the whole project. It helps if you keep the project story to hand and repeat it constantly to establish exactly what the project really is. Then the team decides on the strategy for the sprint.

The sprint backlog
This is where you should formulate more precisely (some of) the roughly sketched items that were put in the project backlog. Take the most important items

for the first sprint, and define when you as a team believe that you are satisfied with the quality of the work. This is called 'the definition of done'. Remember that the backlog is not a fixed list of interventions, as in the old communication plan. The backlog is a living document. Some items stay, others will change or be dropped from the backlog because of progressive insight. Do not kill what you drop, just freeze it, and choose what you think appropriate from the remaining interventions in the project backlog. Experience teaches that there will surely be plenty to choose from. The rest remains in the project backlog for a possible pick-up in later stages. Finally, working with the Scrum method means that your interventions should at all times be 'light' and easy to adjust.

Alliances

You may very well need to think about alliances with other people or departments. Or perhaps you need a person or external party who is familiar with your project target group, so-called intermediaries with whom you can cooperate or who can assist you to take your message further. One basic Scrum rule says: 'never do things alone when you can do them together'.

To do list

And of course you have to create a work program which securely defines who is doing what and what facilities are required. In IT the team normally stays together throughout the project. In our experiments in the Netherlands we have noted that this is not always the case in our field. In these circumstances the Scrum master needs to keep an extra eye on team building.

/ Building block 4a: **Sprint**

Then the implementation can begin. The RCS method is stringent in terms of method. How much time a sprint may take, who is going to do what and how often the team will get together for a stand-up scrum meeting are all precisely decided in advance.

What is a sprint?

The sprint embodies the progress of the project. This is where actions take place. I prefer to use the word interventions rather than actions, so from here on I will use 'interventions'. A sprint is a fixed period of one to four weeks, although I know of very short term projects in which the sprints lasted for only one day. The general premise is: shorter sprints are better sprints.

Teamwork

The core of Scrum is a self-steering team, who themselves do everything that needs to be done during the sprint. Together they are responsible and together they make decisions on how to complete the sprint in a satisfactory manner. That is why the size of a team is important: seven plus or minus two is ideal. A team must be as multidisciplinary as is necessary to fulfill the ambition. Thus an ambition may very well dictate that a designer, a copywriter, a campaign planner and a spokesperson should definitely be among the members of the team. Or other disciplines, you name it. To finish the sprint properly it may even be essential to recruit external specialists to literally sit in.

Progress
The Scrum master closely monitors progress. The Scrum master is best seen as a project manager, but without the authority to make decisions. The team works independently, so there is no boss. Team decisions are based on consensus and, if necessary, assisted by the Scrum master, since it is his or her responsibility to ensure that work is not interrupted by any obstacles, such as insufficient support from outsiders, misunderstandings, differences of opinion and so on.

So the Scrum master follows the team's progress meticulously in order to safeguard a realistic and smooth operation. And where appropriate, he or she consults the project owner or the client herself.

Documentation
Of course, the team must keep a record for itself and for the stakeholders of what everyone is doing. But Scrum means minimal documentation. For that reason documentation is by means of a so-called sprint chart, dashboard or a board on the wall where the team sticks Post-its giving short task descriptions and a name tag. Priorities are shown at the top of the board. Whatever is on hold is recorded on the left side of the board, with what's being currently worked on in the middle segment and what's finished shown in the right column. Ideas and alternatives usually emerge in the process, but these must be rigorously deposited in the project backlog for consideration in a later sprint.

/ Building block 4b: **Scrum**

The team meets on a regular basis to 'scrum'. In software development practice it addresses three questions: what did you do, where did you run into problems, if any, and what are you planning to do between now and the next stand-up? In the field of communication one can safely assume that things are a bit more complicated.

Stand-up meeting
During the daily stand-up scrum the team quickly reviews the progress of all agreed items, challenges what the monitors say, and discusses what is to be done before the next stand-up and what the impediments could be. First, it is important not to allow scrums to exceed 15 minutes. For that reason it is advisable to scrum standing up. And no coffee! Experience has shown that this produces time savings of 50%. A suggestion: give everyone a red card that may be raised if someone speaks too long, or does not comply with the most important purpose of the

scrum: the only useful contribution is what promotes the progress of the current sprint, nothing else.

Monitoring

The core of the RCS method is the ongoing evaluation. It is a most efficient way to check how well the team is doing. Monitoring helps you to estimate how reliable and realistic the actual situation is. It is very important to question what is going on inside and outside the organization, and of course how these issues could influence or have an effect on the success of your project. Equally important are questions about the topic of the sprint itself: how do people talk about its nature and purpose, do these social stories change over time, and if so, how and why? All these social stories together constitute the social mood on the theme of the project, and 'mood' is generally quite critical for success.

Personal reflections

Personal reflections by the members of the team are an important source of information during the stand-ups, since they prompt all kinds of reaction along with the development and implementation of their interventions. Personal reflections are therefore a valuable aid to interpreting the monitors properly. And again, the Scrum master must ensure that members do not take too much time to express their findings. Beware: the team may draw the red card! Any new idea emerging from the stand-ups should not immediately be executed, but filed in the project backlog for consideration for the next sprint(s).

How frequent

In software development Scrum law dictates holding a scrum every day, preferably in the morning. In our field it is questionable whether this regime is appropriate in the majority of cases.

/ Building block 5: **Validation**

At the end of each sprint a validation meeting is set up to assess the value of the interventions that were performed during that sprint and look back at the process. Participants in the meeting must be the project owner, the Scrum master, the team members and possibly some of the stakeholders. The dates are set in advance, so there is no excuse.

Function of the Scrum master
Just like the stand-up scrum meeting, the validation meeting is the responsibility of the Scrum master. The agenda of the validation meeting is all about looking back. First: what are the results of our sprint? Did we achieve our goals? Are we satisfied, and are the project owner and our stakeholders satisfied, too? What can we show him or her to test what we did? Second: what have we done, how did it go and what were the obstacles occurring or recurring in the team? This is called review and retrospective.

Looking Back

During the sprint, the team reflects briefly in the daily scrums. In the validation meeting there is much more time. If the monitors show that the interventions were appropriate, and stakeholders and project owner agree, and the team decides that their working habits are efficient and effective, the sprint is deemed to be valid. That is why I prefer to call this a 'validation meeting'. The Scrum master ensures that solid analyses of the data of the monitors, the process and the teamwork are available. Not in lengthy documents, as Scrum is not eager to allow that, but in an infographic or some other visual tool. Short and simple.

It is also very important to take another look at the ambition of the project and the project story. Do they still stand up against reality as experienced during the sprint? The ambition may very well need to be adjusted one way or the other.

In both scrum and validation meetings it is at the discretion of the Scrum master to invite or allow some 'lookers-on' to assess what the team is doing and to make it more valuable.

Next sprint planning

When a follow-up sprint is necessary, it is best to start the planning directly following the validation meeting. There the following question needs to be answered: what are we going to do in the next sprint? The iteration thus starts all over again and a new sprint backlog is filled.

Usually a follow-up sprint is more efficient than the previous one. Familiarity and experience are a tremendous help.

Reflective Communication Scrum

/ 20 Essentials of the RCS

- Four roles
- Four meetings
- Four artefacts
- Four types of evaluation
- Four forms of accountability

3

/ Four roles

Scrum is all about the people. This alone makes working with methods such as Scrum so enjoyable, according to the experts.

The project owner

In books on project management a great emphasis s usually put on the client. This is all the more emphatically the case in Scrum. Scrum says: Without a client there is no project. In Scrum the client or his agent is effectively committed to the whole process, and as such has the title of project owner. He or she effectively takes part in the Intake, Sprint planning and Validation meetings. The project owner 'owns' the backlogs, and as such decides on what the team will do (of course advised by the members of the team). The project owner works closely with the Scrum master, who brings the project owner up to date on a regular basis. The Scrum master should also have constant access to the project owner to discuss acute problems or obstacles that could endanger the progress of the sprint process. If the project owner is sufficiently committed she must be prepared to accept that this can lead to time-consuming interventions. That is part of the game, so to speak.

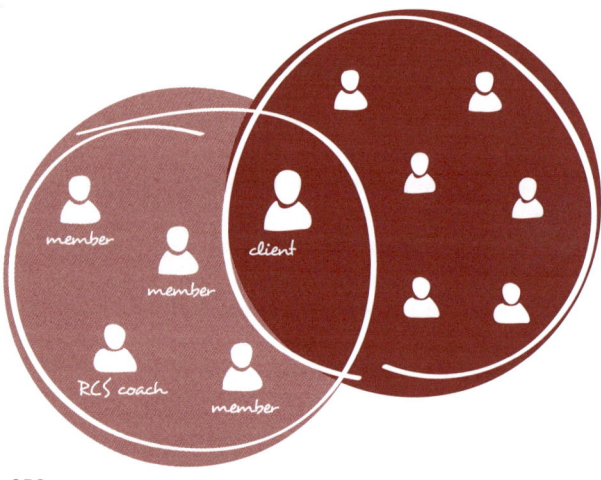

Reflective Communication Scrum

The Scrum master

The project owner decides on what is to happen. The team determines how it will happen. But a team cannot do without a Scrum master. The Scrum master is definitely not the leader or boss – for that is the team itself - but he or she must facilitate, ensuring that the project owner and specific stakeholders stay involved, that other stakeholders are kept informed or stimulated to participate as observers, that meetings are organized and that obstacles are removed. The Scrum master makes sure that the team will become a true team and remain so, and helps the team to act with agility and adhere to the rules of Scrum. The Scrum master is in effect pivotal in the whole process. Implementing Scrum is change management, says Michael Franken in the Dutch version of Scrum for Dummies. This should not be taken lightly. Knowing what the intention is does not necessarily mean being able to carry it out.

The development team

The development team is self-managing, deciding jointly how to go about things. It is entrepreneurial, assertive, communicative and creative. In all circumstances specialist members of the team must be 'T-shaped'. They must be confident solid professionals (the vertical part of the 'T') in combination with the talent to work closely together with birds of other kinds of professional feathers (the horizontal part of the 'T'). This T-shaped personal professionalism forms the pillar of flexible cooperation. These are the key qualities characteristic of the team members.

The team must be as multidisciplinary as required for bringing the project to a successful completion. Manning the team should be defined by the interventions of the sprint. This has nothing to do with functions but all the more with competencies. The backbone of any sprint process is: the participation of the expertise required to achieve the ambition. This means

Four roles

for instance that a team may comprise a copywriter, designer or web designer, a consultant, a sales person or someone from HR, or any other expert, or even a member of the final users, just for the team to be able to meet all challenges dictated by the diversity of the tasks and ambition of the sprint. When they are needed, subcontracted professionals must literally be part of the team and all of its dynamics. They must become true team partners.

The project stakeholders
Last but not least, the stakeholders of the project. One of the stakeholder groups is the 'users' of the interventions. The President of the Agile Consortium, Arie van Bennekum, once said: 'Make the users an accomplice'. For a long time now we, in the field of communication, have borrowed the term 'target group' from the marketing world. But in our business, one rarely knows in advance what the audience (or users group) will be like or, in other words, who will be participating in the communication processes on this particular theme. So, it might be your target group, but it is disputable whether this group will pay you any attention. And the term target group has nothing to do with making them committed. It is for that reason that I prefer to call them stakeholders rather than 'target groups', although I also like the term 'participants'. For us, there's not much more we can do than try to get hold of the stakeholders' social stories and connect with these or adapt them to our aims.

But there's more to say about stakeholders. Other parties may be essential in an RCS trajectory: marketing expertise if the theme relates closely to marketing, or finance, legal or HR. It may be very useful to involve them, try to engage them or at least keep them informed. And it is very often useful to involve external organizations or networks, for instance representatives of the proposed stakeholders or even of rival organizations.

now take a more
...s in the Scrum
...ily scrum and

...onal Scrum
...e project, but only,
if at all, as a Sprint 0. Another agile project delivery framework, DSDM (Dynamic Systems Development Method), recognizes three phases: pre-project, project life cycle and the post-project phase, where the purpose is to ensure that the system is still operating effectively. In the pre-project phase candidate projects are identified, project funding has been obtained and project commitment is ensured. In the first steps of the project life cycle a feasibility study and a business study are complementary.

I borrowed these notions of DSDM to be discussed and decided on in Intake meetings. Addressing these issues at an early stage avoids problems at later stages of the project, DSDM claims. In these meeting(s) the assignment of the project can be completed, the story defining or redefining the goal of the project can be created, the project owner can decide on the required competencies in the team, and the project backlog can be designed. Please note that in agile working all these decisions are to be challenged during the process: Responding to change over following the plan. 'Accept that functionality is flexible', Jeff Sutherland et al. say in *The Power of Scrum* (page 48): 'It's going to change. It can't be frozen up front. Once you accept that, then you can nail down quality, cost and time.'

Sprint planning
Only after the Intake phase can the Scrum iterations or sprints be started. In the Sprint planning meeting the Sprint goal is decided on, the Sprint backlog is

produced and the items in the backlog are prioritized. A sprint normally lasts for 1 - 4 weeks. In this phase the goals can be specified in more detail than for the project as a whole. Goals can relate to the results of the sprint as well as to the working practices of the team.

The Sprint planning meeting first decides what the team can cover, considering the time it has available during the sprint. The most important items of the project backlog are then identified for working on during the sprint. MoSCoW is an acronym used in DSDM that represents a way of prioritizing requirements. It stands for:
- MUST have this requirement to meet the business needs
- SHOULD have this requirement if at all possible, but the project's success does not rely on this
- COULD have this requirement if it does not affect the fitness of business needs of the project
- WON'T represents a requirement that stakeholders have agreed will not be implemented in a given release, but may be considered for the future.

When the most important items are put in the sprint backlog, the relative weight of the items is then discussed. Scrum professionals usually do that with a poker game that combines fun with efficiency. Instead of calculating the resources needed to accomplish the item, the team gives estimates that are relative to each other. The true value of planning poker lies in the discussion, not in the numbers. For beginner Scrum teams it might be helpful to work with man-hours to estimate the workload of a sprint.

Daily scrum
During the sprint the Scrum master organizes the daily stand- up in such a way that the team members can discuss what they are doing and what they intend to do, and are able to do their day's work in the most

Four meetings

efficient and effective way. The daily stand-up has only one very clear goal, Jeff Sutherland et al. say: 'How can we have the best and most effective day possible as a team?' To do that people in IT are asked three questions, as said. 1: What have you done since the last stand-up? 2: What will you achieve before the next stand-up? 3: What's getting in your way?

I prefer to exchange and discuss four questions in the daily (or every other day) scrums in corporate communication and public relations and I prefer a different sequence:
1. What have we done since the last stand-up?
2. What can we learn from the monitors and our personal reflections?
3. What is getting in our way?
4. What will we achieve before the next stand-up?

We have noticed that in corporate communication and public relations the monitors and personal reflections may show that what the team is doing is no longer relevant. In that case the daily scrum leads to cancellation of the sprint. The Scrum master then immediately discusses the question of earlier sprint validation with the project owner.

Sprint validation
Sprint validation marks the closure of the sprint. Since the length of the sprint is always fixed, the meeting can be scheduled upfront. In the validation meeting the participants take a more structured look at the sprint than they do during the daily stand-ups. If the monitors show that the interventions were appropriate and stakeholders and the project owner agree, and the team decides that their working habits are efficient and effective, the sprint is deemed to be valid, and if not, other interventions or working habits are considered to make the project successful.
The Scrum master ensures that solid analyses are available of monitoring data, the process and team-

work. Not in lengthy documents, as Scrum is not keen to permit these, but in an infographic or some other visual tool. Short and simple.

It is also very important to take a good look at the ambition decided on in the Intake meeting. Does it still hold against reality as experienced during the sprint? The ambition may very well need to be adjusted one way or the other. Responding to change prevails over following a plan, as the Agile Manifesto claims. The team and the project owner have to decide on that together, assisted by the Scrum master.

It is at the discretion of the Scrum master to invite or allow some 'lookers-on' to both Scrum and validation meetings, purely to keep them informed. At no time are such observers permitted to take part in the discussion. The Scrum master is responsible for making sure of that.

/ **Four artefacts**

Artefacts in Scrum are the means used to make visible what is agreed upon and what the results are. Artefacts replace lengthy documents and, as such, the project archives.

Project story
It is extremely important that the project owner, the development team and the Scrum master have a common story on what the project entails, what stakeholders find really important, and how they reflect on all this. Although this is not part of the original Scrum method, we have seen in our projects in the Netherlands that an essential part of building the project and the team is to create a shared story of the project and its ambitions, and hang it on the Scrum wall. As soon as the project story has been created and written down, it helps to build up the project backlog.

Project backlog
The project backlog is started up in the Intake phase. A project backlog is a prioritized features list, containing brief descriptions of all functionality desired in the project. In IT these are often called 'user stories', the features users see as important. I prefer to call the backlog the 'repertoire' of the project: all the work that needs to be done to achieve the project ambitions. It is preferable to define these in terms of what stakeholders find important. Thus not as: 'write a brochure', but 'provide stakeholders with clear and understandable document on the issue in an agreeable form'.

When applying Scrum, it's not necessary to start a project with a lengthy, upfront effort to document all requirements and all actions designed to meet the requirements. Typically, a Scrum team and its project owner start by writing down everything they can think of for agile backlog prioritization. What they come up with is almost always more than enough for a first sprint. The Scrum project backlog is then allowed to grow and change as more is learned about the project and its stakeholders.

Some Scrum professionals prefer to work with the Iceberg model: Below sea level you have the vague long-term ambitions of the project, while above you have all the interventions that can be realized in one to three sprints. In between are ambitions that are more concrete than in the list below but too vague to start with.

Sprint backlog
A sprint backlog is a list of the interventions and requirements to be completed within the sprint. When working with the Iceberg Model, you choose the items from above sea level. Normally, the sprint backlog consists of two to six items. So they should not be too detailed.

After choosing the items, the team starts to estimate the relative effort for each item. I referred to when discussing the Sprint meeting on pages 48-49. For every item the team defines its 'Definition of Done'. The Scrum Guide™ describes the Definition of Done (DoD) as a tool for bringing transparency to the work a Scrum team is performing. It is related more to the quality of a product, rather than to its functionality. During the Sprint planning meeting, the Scrum team develops or reconfirms its DoD, which lets the members of the team know how much work to select for a given Sprint. The team writes the DoDs on the wall next to the items, and makes the results they are satisfied with as smart as possible.

The team then divides every item into specific tasks. The item 'Provide stakeholders with clear and understandable document on the issue in an agreeable form' will be divided into quite a number of tasks such as: 'decide on a specific format', 'ask bids from

/ Four artefacts

a printing company', 'write a text', 'find illustrations' and so on. Finally the team estimates the effort (in hours) needed to complete each task and meet the DoD.

Showable results

Last but not least: Scrum is very result-oriented and Scrum teams are always very eager to have even minor results as soon as possible. A result is not the final part of the project, as in classic project management. Instead, everything a team does in a sprint is seen as a result, something that can be shown and tested, refined if necessary, and considered as another stepping stone towards realizing the project ambitions. The team will produce a dummy to show to the project owner and some stakeholders in order to test the idea and so on. The end-result of the project is consequently no more than the sum of all the showable and refined results from the sprints.

/ Evaluation

In the traditional corporate communication or public relations planning methods the emphasis is on accountability in retrospect, at the end of the project. In the evaluation theory this is termed summative evaluation. Moreover, the intention is to be as accurate as possible in measuring whether the predetermined objectives have been achieved. And if so, in what way, and if not, what the causal factors may have been. In addition to evaluating the impact you can also verify whether staff and resources were efficiently deployed, or how the process developed and whether that was efficient and effective. This is all about summative evaluation. In both the professional literature and in practice evaluation is almost invariably taken to be similar to reporting accountability in retrospect. Some authors moreover believe evaluation is impossible if no targets have been set in the first place.

However that alone does not cover evaluation theory. Evaluation theory is much more generous. It embraces more than one type of evaluation, and I believe that these sometimes offer more insight and are more likely to produce positive results than by only evaluating after the event. I describe the different forms of evaluation on the following pages.

The question remains whether you can simply evaluate the communication effect itself (the output) or should (also) focus on the contribution of communication to resolving the original problem (the outcome). This is an important addition, because a communication issue usually does not arise on its own. Its assessment should therefore basically be done with the overall picture in mind. But all that is often laborious to demonstrate or prove because how would you know what to attribute to communication? What might be due to actions by other parties, or simply to a change in social mood or a sudden action by a competitor?

/ **Evaluation Model**

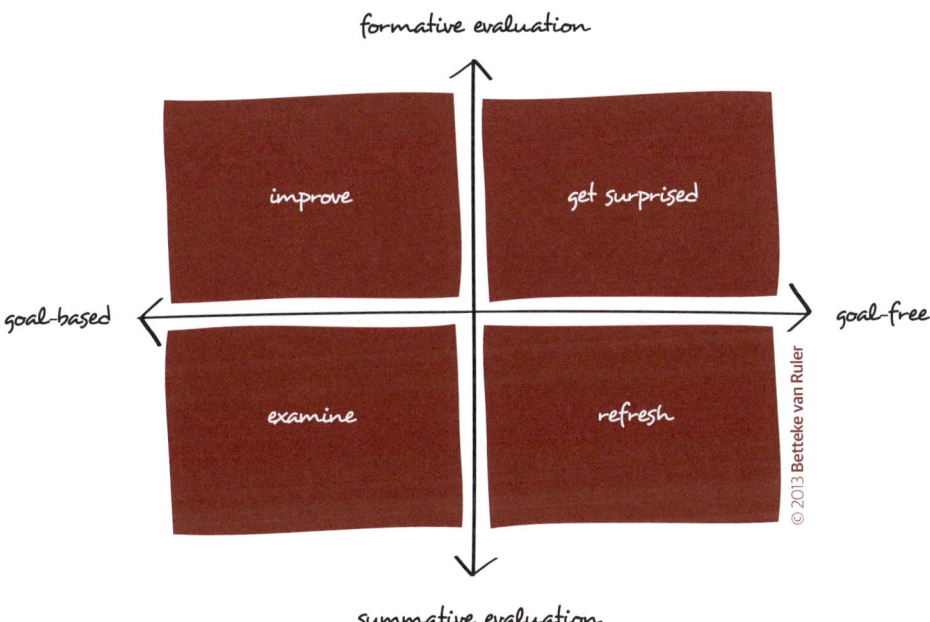

/ **Four types of evaluation**

In daily practice, an evaluation is usually meant to check whether objectives have been achieved. Michael Scriven, the methodology scholar, calls that goal-based: aimed at measuring the difference between the original target/goal and the end result.

Goal-free evaluation
Michael Scriven recommends also evaluating goal-free, whereby assessment is based on very different standards, such as whether a particular intervention is in line with relevant theories, whether the chosen interventions are morally acceptable, or how the dynamics in the environment are of any influence. Goal-free evaluation helps you to detect the unexpected. That is, if you are not overly determined to cling to your own personal reference. This is called 'self-referentiality', and is based on selective perception: people tend to specifically filter information from the environment that they themselves deem to be useful and do not perceive as threatening. As a result they see certain things while others remain invisible. Self-referentiality is the pitfall of goal-free evaluation.

The unexpected
Thorough goal-free evaluation calls for looking at the unexpected and is consequently a matter of opening up mental blinds and taking on a broad perspective. To do that you need to be able to think critically and take predictions and well-intentioned advice from a learning perspective, Nassim Talib says in his book *The Black Swan*. And 'Learn to make an omelet with broken eggs': i.e. do not try to glue the eggshell together again but do something else with it. That also requires entrepreneurship and freedom of action. Goal-free evaluation is a basic element of the Reflective Communication Scrum.

Formative evaluation
Evaluation theory distinguishes furthermore between summative and formative assessment. Formative

Ken Schwaber in Agile Project Management with Scrum

'Most people responsible for managing projects have been taught a deterministic approach to project management that uses detailed plans, Gantt charts and work schedules. Scrum is the exact opposite.'

/ **Table of Contents**

Reflective Communication Scrum

008	Introduction
015	Chapter 1 | **A new way of planning**
033	Chapter 2 | **This is how you do it**
055	Chapter 3 | **5 x 4 Essentials of the RCS**
074	Chapter 4 | **Backgrounds of the RCS**
088	Glossary
090	List of references

/ **Introduction**

Reflective Communication Scrum is a new methodology for planning communication actions. Its execution is governed by strict rules, but none of the content, i.e. what you do, is prescribed in advance. The characteristics of Scrum methodology are defined as: strict adherence to the rules and flexibility regarding content.

In traditional corporate communication or public relations planning the results you will obtain (in smart objectives) and the actions needed to achieve your objectives are precisely defined. Changing conditions along the way, or proof of any unanticipated negative effects of your actions will impel you to admit in hindsight that your goals had not been realistic, that you had aimed at the wrong targets or that you had not had the right strategy or taken the correct actions, and that your actions had therefore been misconstrued. In short: a waste of (most of your) time and money.

Many communication professionals encounter these problems and are tempted to deviate from their communication plan, or drop it altogether. But it's a case of 'no plan, no future', as the saying goes. It is clear that one simply must keep track of things, otherwise you risk losing your way in any process. **Most people need some sort of a lead or a map for reference and at least some generalized objectives.** Otherwise any incident that occurs will force you to improvise and probably take you further off course as a result. That is, if you can still see any course. If you are about to lose focus because of changes along the way, chaos is a real threat. So instead of an unrealistic plan you need a method to provide structure to your thoughts, to give direction and to determine priorities. Planning methodology helps you to justify decisions and be accountable regarding manpower, money, choices and so on. It also dissuades you from thinking solely about doing things, taking action. But such a method must be equal to the challenges of the unpredictability and dynamics in the realm of professional and strategic communication.

Reflective Communication Scrum is just such a method. RCS not only embraces flexibility, but also justifies it by using ongoing evaluation to gain insights for decision-making. That is why it is called Scrum for *reflective communication*. People who scrum are excited about it. They rave about its natural intensity of cooperation, the genuine urge to get things done in the shortest possible time, the rapid results you can get and the facilitating position of the Scrum master (who is sometimes also called team leader, or facilitator. We call her the Scrum master). Last but not least, they favor the central role of the client, or his representative, here called the 'project owner'. All of which makes work much more fun while delivering much better results. It is therefore no surprise that the Scrum method is on a rapid rise all over the world.

Scrum was conceived by two Japanese scientists, Ikujiro Nonaka and Hirotaka Takeuchi, as a result of their research about the competitive Japanese automotive industry in the 1980s. Those corporations who led the field used a very flexible project planning method. Nonaka and Takeuchi called it 'Scrum'. Much later the software industry adopted it and developed it further to achieve its popular perfection of today. Today you will see Scrum also applied in other fields: in online communication, website development, marketing, finance, HR management, E-health, organizational change, policy making and so on.

After many experiences with Scrum experts and professionals in the communication business, and having read many books and websites on Scrum, I'm sure Scrum answers the demands of the new reality of communication management. First of all because even unforeseen dynamics and complexity are no longer seen as obstacles. They are cleverly accommodated in the method. Second, because the time has passed that it was only after the event, if at all, that you had to justify your choices and decisions. With this method, you are automatically accountable throughout the method. It comes with the territory. And who would not want that? In Scrum the team is always self-steering and multi-disciplinary. Creativity, entrepreneurship and cooperation are the keywords. The performances of members are closely monitored, not to see if they are doing what they've promised, but to check whether their actions are functional, whether what they do makes a constructive difference for the project as such and the team as a whole.

In Scrum a project is divided into sprints, brief time-fixed periods of one to four weeks. During a sprint, every day – or every other day, whichever seems appropriate – the team discusses its progression during a 15-minute stand-up meeting (the daily scrum) to reflect on what its members have done and will do, what is going on in the outside world and whether those two things fit together. After each sprint the project owner (and other stakeholders if desired) joins the team to evaluate results and process. The project owner – always a mandated delegate of the client and in IT called product owner – is actively involved in and committed to the Scrum project, participates in planning and evaluation meetings and decides on the priorities. In short: he 'owns' the project and thus keeps a close eye on it.

Do not expect this booklet to provide all the answers to questions concerning Scrum practices in the communication business. Scrum is a new phenomenon in communication and at this time simply too fresh to yield a comprehensive range of experiences. In this booklet I attempt to adapt the method to benefit the needs of communication professionals in their daily work. I believe that together we can refine the method and start to identify best practices so as to tailor the method for the benefit of all communication professionals.

Betteke van Ruler
www.bettekevanruler.nl

/ **What's the use of RCS?**

> Hi Stephen, what do you think of Scrum?

> So, we need to align with modern demands?

> Do you think that Scrum is only for projects with a typical final product, like a conference or an advertising campaign? Or will it be suitable for other public relations efforts, too?

> Knowledge scholars are talking about the change from routine expertise to reflective or adaptive expertise. Do we need to include these types of expertise into our toolkits?

> What kind of competencies do we need to pilot new approaches and structures?

> Thanks Stephen!

Betteke van Ruler *Emeritus Professor of Communication Studies University of Amsterdam.*

The dominant workflow in public relations is more than 100 years old. It's no longer fit for purpose in a real time always on world.

Yes, we need to redevelop our processes and systems.

In my view there is an opportunity to use the Scrum approach in any situation where you're able to define a clear objective with a measurable outcome. That could be an ongoing public relations program just as easily as a discrete project.

A shift to a more agile approach that is suited to modern forms of engagement is critical to our future. We need to pilot new approaches and structure within our teams. I'm a huge believer in fast failure and rapid iterative development.

We need to be brave enough to recognize that our existing structures are no longer fit for purpose. We also need to recognize that we can't start from scratch and that we need to transition from old models to new. That requires bravery and starts with pilots at the edges of communication programs.

Stephen Waddington *@wadds is European Digital & Social Media Director Ketchum*

evaluation focuses on the team's awareness of what they are doing and/or improving their actions. In communication practice this is sometimes called process evaluation, but it does not necessarily have to relate to the process. It can equally well be addressing the question of whether the team is on course, or actions need to be improved. In these cases we are talking about goal-based formative assessment. Looking at the unexpected to make informed decisions equals goal-free formative evaluation. In RCS both types of evaluation are required in daily scrums.

Regular monitoring

Formative evaluation means deploying monitors to search for the dynamics in the environment, for changes in the force field, and for the social stories about important issues. The latter not being the least receptive to dynamics: our views on things change almost daily due to social mood swings. Our personal environment suddenly seems to think differently as a result of something that appears unexpectedly, or our mood swings simply because the fridge just went on the blink. So it makes no sense to only investigate beforehand and then assume that you know the truth for the duration of your project. Regular monitoring is a must. It is the only way to keep track of changes and thus on development.

Quantitative or qualitative

Summative assessment is usually quantitative, whereas formative assessment is usually qualitative. The difference? If you just want to know how often something occurs, you evaluate quantitatively. If you want to know about the nature of a phenomenon, you evaluate qualitatively. Many professionals prefer quantitative research, as it provides numbers. It is easy, and managers love numbers, they say. Qualitative research however produces much deeper and more relevant information. So both matter.

/ **Four aspects of accountability**

Professional accountability | Decisional & Social accountability

Accountability is concerned with responsibility to someone or for some activity. It means on the one hand being responsible for certain things, and on the other, showing others what you have done or are doing. Accountability is a key component in all stages of the Reflective Communication Scrum: In the first stage, it's all in the professionalism of the team members to shape and give substance to the ambition. After that it shows in the quality of the choices made, and finally in taking responsibility for the results.

Professional accountability
The fact is, unlike what ought to be the case, that we typically fail to include individual professionalism in the concept of accountability. Professionalism entails an awareness of what you are doing stems from professional knowledge and norms. That is the aspect of accountability that is concerned with taking responsibility. For professional accountability you need a clear vision on and knowledge of your profession, and you need to have the guts to take a firm stand on what must be done first and what comes after. It's the priorities that you choose that earn you roughly the first 50% of your credit.

Decisional accountability
Because of the poor predictability of communication actions, academics point to the importance of focusing on the foundation of choices made in the process rather than on the eventual results. This is done by researching and studying the current situation and utilizing theories that have offered solace in similar situations. Based on monitoring, applying theories and discussing all you see and hear, you gain insights.

vision   *intake*   *kick-off*

Reflective Communication Scrum

Performative accountability

That augments the quality of your choices. Fundamental choices in the RCS basically take place in the sprint planning meetings and daily scrums.

Social accountability

In addition to doing research and studying theory, it is also important to think about whether you make the right moral choices. Communication in and between organizations always has a moral dimension. The inhouse style of communicating between each other determines the mutual relationships and responsibilities and consequently the 'style of the house'. To the outside world that inhouse style determines the associations and emotions that the organization evokes with suppliers and customers in the industry and in the media, as Rob van Es, a scholar on ethics, claims. Every choice therefore needs not only a theoretical and an empirical, but also a moral underpinning. Scholars call that social accountability.

Performative accountability

The best-known form of accountability is demonstrating what you have achieved after the event. Anything you can show afterwards is fine, and welcome, but when that's your only form of accountability, you're most probably in for trying times. With the RCS those days are over. That's because the client is brought on board for the whole process and participates in decisions made in the Intake, Sprint planning and Validation meetings. Which means that afterwards there is nothing to defend: everything has been instantly validated during the Scrum process.

Reflective Communication Scrum

/ A new way of planning

> The more dynamic the environment, the more flexible the plan
>
> Scrum embraces and formalizes this flexibility
>
> It is all about cooperation, entrepreneurship and creativity

/ **The traditional planning method**

diagnosis
⬇
target groups
⬇
objectives
⬇
strategy
⬇
tactics
⬇
evaluation

In the various editions of his well-known book *Strategic Planning for Public Relations*, R.D. Smith suggests that the planning process in public relations consists of four phases with altogether nine steps. The first phase is analysis of the situation, the organization and the publics. The second is to draw up a strategic plan, which means establishing goals and objectives, formulating action and response strategies and developing the message strategy. The third phase is tactics, which means first selecting communication tactics, and then implementing the strategic plan. The fourth phase is evaluation of the plan.
This method is also known as RACE: Research, Action plan, Communication, Evaluation.

All too linear
In this kind of traditional communication planning you determine beforehand what results you want to achieve and what actions you must perform to arrive there. You set your targets and tactics in advance.

When conditions change along the way, or when the effects of your actions prove to be different to what you expected, you are forced to admit that your goals were not realistic, that you had aimed at the wrong target and/or that you had not chosen the right strategy, the right actions, or the right message. In short: a waste of money and effort. The traditional planning method is based on the classical theory of scientific management and a rather old-fashioned idea of how to build strategy. In our dynamic and digitized world, these approaches to management and strategy are seen as 'far too linear'. Most books on communication planning leave scant room for adjustments, or only by exception. It is in no way a structural building block of the planning model. So how can it do any good in the dynamic environment in which organizations are living today?

Many plans are merely action plans

In traditional planning methods goals are formulated as the second step and they need to be formulated SMART: Specific, Measurable, Acceptable, Realistic, Time-bound. This is done to make it possible to show what you've accomplished at the end of the project. That implies that the effects of communication are assumed to be predictable. Many communication professionals therefore rightly refrain from formulating specific objectives. But then, by doing so, there is little left to evaluate afterwards. Some practitioners do not mind. But if evaluation is not deemed necessary, communication is in fact seen as a magic bullet. A magic bullet which, if properly orchestrated (usually with a core message) and smartly distributed, may well ensure success. That is a pre-scientific approach to communication, and also to planning. Such a plan is by no means a strategic communication plan. It should merely be labeled an action plan.

Communication is not all that powerful

Of course, everyone knows it's not that simple. It is simply not the case that 'if only you knew what

I know, you would have the same idea'. Yet I often see corporate communication and public relations plans promising specific effects, greater knowledge, or changed attitudes or behavior, without answering the question whether these claims can be made in advance and why. If any attention is paid to evaluation, it is only to verify whether the objectives have eventually been achieved. The erratic nature of ideas, attitudes and behavior of target groups are not too often subject of the conversation between professionals. How realistic is that?

In Scrum changes are no obstacles

The traditional communication plan does not take into account the complexity of most communication issues and the dynamics in their context. If circumstances change, communication professionals too readily regard these changes as obstacles and consequently as natural excuses for objectives not being achieved.

Most professionals therefore indeed produce a communication plan – as is expected of them - and almost immediately put it aside because it is outdated the moment they have completed it. Is it then not better to replace it and have a method which by nature embraces dynamics and change?

Dwight D. Eisenhower

'Plans are nothing,
planning is everything.'

/ **A planning method**

/ Arranges and structures your activities
/ Helps you to concentrate on ends and results
/ Substantiates whatever you need
/ Legitimizes your activities, your budget and your commitment
/ Shows you where to align, with whom to collaborate
/ Helps you to stay on track
/ Keeps you away from relying on means and tactics

So a method is useful!

/ **The Scrum method**

/ Disciplined method
/ Customized implementation
/ Regular reflections in recurrent sessions
/ Continuous involvement of the client
/ Built-in attention to dynamics
/ Joint responsibility
/ Co-creation with stakeholders

Japanese scientists Nonaka and Takeuchi devised Scrum as a planning method. In Harvard Business Review in 1986 they described how projects gave better results when executed by small, flexible and closely collaborating self-steering teams. They christened it 'Scrum'. Scrum is a term from rugby football to describe a formation of opposing teams fighting for the ball after a foul. In Scrum thinking there are two kinds of approaches, or 'schools' if you wish: the hardliners (everything must be exactly according to the rules of the method), and the moderates. I am a supporter of the latter. I prefer functionality above all else. A method is just a handle, and if a method does not provide the best result, then adjust the method. As long as the method is agile, it is fine to me.

Immensely popular

Scrum has been growing immensely in popularity in recent years. Nowadays there are many training courses to become a Certified Scrum Master, Product Owner or just a Scrum Professional. Scrum is spreading rapidly. The basis of Scrum is iterative planning based on agility. This is well known in crisis communication and in press relations, and seems to work well in these areas. When using agile methods like Scrum, it is more important to accommodate change than to adhere to a strict plan. In a highly dynamic environment, which most organizations have nowadays, this works better than a static plan with predefined results and tactics.

Work differently

Scrum is a specific way of working, not directed from above with an embedded plan but instead with self-steering teams of specialists who are constantly looking for the best actions to take to solve problems and shoot obstacles out of the way.

When to Scrum?

You don't need Scrum when the projects or problems are small and fairly predictable. Scrum is best suited to situations where the outcome is not predictable in advance and the context is complex. But isn't every project complex these days?

Pieter Jongerius et al. in *Get Agile!*

'Scrum is a radical different way of working: as many activities as possible take place at the same time, in the same room. Scrum has many advantages: projects are completed quicker, product quality is higher and the deliverance guarantee is much greater than if using traditional project methods.'

/ **The RCS Building blocks**

①
Building block 1/
Vision

The method relies foremost on the people assigned to the project. They determine its success.
In order to act as a professional team member it is crucial for team members to have a clear vision of their own professionalism.
In short: on priorities from their professional point of view.
The only way to develop a sharp vision is to challenge it and talk to each other about it.

②
Building block 2/
Intake

During the intake the project owner, the Scrum master and a preliminary team discuss the assignment. In this phase the project ambitions are settled, the project backlog is created, settlements are made for the budget, more team members are requested if necessary, and the project backlog is filled. Finally, the length of the sprints is determined as well as the timing of the daily stand-up scrums.

③
Building block 3/
Sprint planning

In sprint planning the team chooses carefully what the focus should be of the sprint, which strategies are most appropriate to address the issues/items for this sprint and achieve the sprint's goals. It decides on a realistic number of defined items from the backlog and decides on the definition of some of these items.

Handwritten annotations:
- Prioritized features list; short descriptions (pointing to "project backlog")
- Roadmap + requirements are foundation for the backlog

4 ......
Building block 4/
Sprint and scrum

The sprint is a predetermined period during which the proposed actions are developed and implemented. During the daily scrum the team quickly reviews the progress of all agreed items, challenges what the monitors say, and discusses what is to be done until the next stand-up and what the team's impediments could be.

5 ......
Building block 5/
Validation

After each sprint, a validation meeting is held with the project owner and possibly other stakeholders to evaluate the results and the process. It may be necessary to discuss the workload for subsequent sprints as well as the habits of the team. It may even be necessary to adjust the ambition of the project itself, based on the outcome of the validation meeting.

6 ......
Building block 6/
Result

The project is complete when the outcome of the last sprint and/or the ambition (perhaps meanwhile adjusted) and the results are in sync, and of course also when the deadline has arrived or no more money is available.

Sweet Scrum: A different taste of doing things

There was buzz in the air, that one morning before a sprint validation meeting. It concerned a big, high-pressured project focused on the reorganization of healthcare services, which I facilitated as a Scrum master. Now word was that a team member, a father of four, had baked cupcakes with his kids' cupcake baking set. As he approached the team, a distinct bakery smell permeated the air and we realized we got lucky. He had decorated the cupcakes in every color of the rainbow, writing on every one of them: 'Sprint 3.' He was as proud of his own bakery skills as he was of the team's results this sprint.

In the years I have worked with Scrum, and the many teams I assisted, the number of cakes and other celebratory indulgences I have seen is pretty unusual. As I look back, I think much of it has to do with the new ways people find to interact within a Scrum setting. In this setting, ordinary concepts often get a new meaning. Like a 'meeting', for example. Do professionals in an ordinary meeting really meet? And are those meetings really enjoyable? As soon as you have experienced a Scrum meeting with your team in which you stand up and can freely share your thoughts, you realize meetings are what you make of them.

Now management books often talk about celebrating your team's victories. But do we really celebrate? And do it often enough? You might know the answer. As you might experience, Scrum celebrates team performance.

Can Scrum be used in an international innovation competition among mayors organized by Michael Bloomberg of New York, involving €9 million in cash prizes? Team Amsterdam would soon find out during the so-called Mayors Challenge 2014.

Having a very demanding mayor as a project owner in a Scrum team is a challenge in itself; how could we make this mayoral innovation pressure cooker fun, facing 181 other competing cities? In true scrum fashion, we used sprints of one week with a tangible result to be delivered every time. This could be a presentation, an app design, a strategy for engaging European cities, et cetera. It was shared at every sprint review, followed by a festive dinner, a retrospective and a new sprint planning. As a consequence, team members would be working well into the night, but their motivation was kept strong by showing results and celebrating them every week.

The high spirits of the team quickly sucked the mayor in. As a project owner he went on to extend these good vibes to the outside world: two big events were organized to which partners, stakeholders and citizens were invited. In the end, project owner and team had grown toward each other during a very unpredictable innovation process. As a result, Amsterdam reached the finals with 20 other cities.

Gidion Peters
Scrum master, Scrum Company

/ **The Agile Manifesto for public relations and corporate communication**

/ Individuals and interactions prevail over processes and tools

/ Functionality prevails over agreed-upon objectives and actions

/ Intense cooperation prevails over commissioning sub-contracting

/ Responding to change prevails over following a plan

☛ See **www.agilemanifesto.org** for the original Agile Manifesto for agile software development.

Scrum is a method for delivering project results, stemming from a philosophy in which the talents of your employees are taken as a reliable benchmark, called agile. It promotes flexibility when dealing with change, there is structural interaction based on trust and it is entirely focused on delivery on time of products or services that really make a difference. Unnecessary documentation is omitted and there is plenty of room for development of fresh insights and realistic alternatives, as agile experts say.

Supporters of the agile way of working depict the traditional planning form scornfully as the 'waterfall' or the 'cascade', because what needs to be done is devised in detail behind the desk and all actions are almost automatically supposed to be executed like a waterfall, without reality checks of its functionalities in that process.

As Dutch agile guru Sander Hoogendoorn says in his book *This is Agile*, most important is the way team members are focused to achieve the best results. The practical details of the method may differ from project to project. Characteristic for agile working is that team members, project owner and possibly other stakeholders work together for optimum results, that hierarchy is out of order and that bureaucracy is restricted to a minimum. Only what really helps to achieve your ambitions and what's really functional is pursued. Changes are not seen as obstacles but on the contrary are welcomed and formalized. Small multi-disciplinary teams work together in short iterations, 'sprints', phased over timeboxes in which the actions are executed. Team members collaborate with each other instead of working one after the other. The team as a whole takes responsibility for the result.

Reflective Communication Scrum

/ Backgrounds of the RCS

- Communication, the basics of the profession
- Reflection as a key concept for a professional
- And much more

4

/ How communication works

Communication is a 'plastic' word: everyone feels comfortable with it and uses it, but not always adequately and seldom explaining what he or she means by it.

Connection
Connection is often seen as the essence of communication in the professional literature. But that does not fully cover human communication. In this perspective on communication the emphasis is mainly on transmission. The most frequently cited model of communication is the Sender - Medium – Channel - Receiver (SMCR) model, which emphasizes the transfer of a message and to some extent the noise nuisance that may occur.

One-way influence
The SMCR model is often widened by the wish to achieve a particular effect, more than just the reception of the message. The formula that is often used in practice to accomplish this is AIDA: Attention - Interest - Desire - Action. However, communication science sees the AIDA formula as too simple. Hence the more complex models, such as Fishbein & Ajzen's Theory of Reasoned Action and the ELM model of Petty & Cacioppo are used in this perspective on how communication works. All intended to search for predictions of predefined attitudes and behavioral intentions. These are commonly seen as models of communication from the perspective of the recipient, not because these models are centered on an active and independent person, but because receiving and processing information is a process that causes the sender much trouble.

Interaction
According to others, communication is only communication if it's a two-way process 'between' people instead of 'from one to the other'. The core of 'interaction-thinking' is grasping what the other

person is concerned about and engaging in a dialogue with him or her. The outcome should not be that the one is affected by the other, but the commencement of a process of listening to each other and having a conversation. This is often complemented by a more relational view: just listening to each other is not enough, agreement is what counts. A prerequisite is that both parties have the same intentions: for 'It takes two to tango', and that is not always the case.

Transaction

There is yet another vision on how communication works, and this one has my preference. So far it is still not very common in communication practice, but it is certainly a very interesting view indeed in our digitized world. It is a vision of communication as a dynamic process of transactions of meanings, which evolves in time and place. Who is going to participate is unknown beforehand. No one knows in advance how the process will turn out and what meanings (concepts, ideas) will develop. That will only unfold during the process.

Attention to dynamics

The American communication philosopher Lee Thayer speaks of communication as a diachronic process: developing over time. As long as an issue is being discussed the meanings given to it remain under construction. Sometimes it is in line with what the initiator desired for an effect, but it might equally be producing unintended effects. I prefer this view of how communication works because how people will think is simply not fixed and depends not only on their personal capacities and feelings. Moreover, in communication you often even do not know who is taking part in that process, and that makes it even more complicated to identify in advance what a smart goal of your project might be. I consequently prefer a transactional, dynamic view of communication, and that is why I prefer Scrum, too.

/ **Acting reflective**

The RCS method is all about reflecting and adjusting. In this I use the thinking of Kurt Lewin concerning reflective action and the similar PDCA model of W. Edwards Deming. All of these approaches inspire me as they pay attention to dynamics and development. They thus fit well with the transactional, dynamic view of communication, which to me is fundamental in agile and Scrum-like project management.

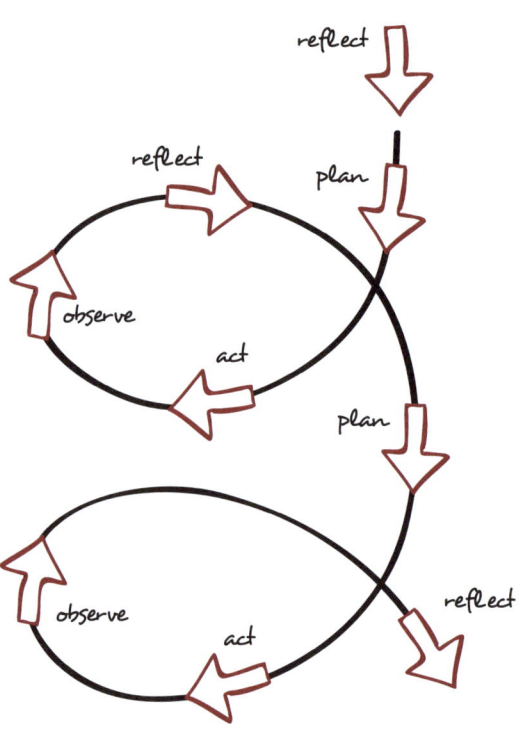

Action Research model

In 1946 Lewin published a frequently cited article in which he argued that professionals continuously reflect on their actions. He was referring to professionals working with minorities, but this applies equally to other professionals. The core idea is that every action must lead to observation of the reaction and reflection on that, to benefit the planning for the following action. This is equivalent to the idea of testing and refinement in Scrum.

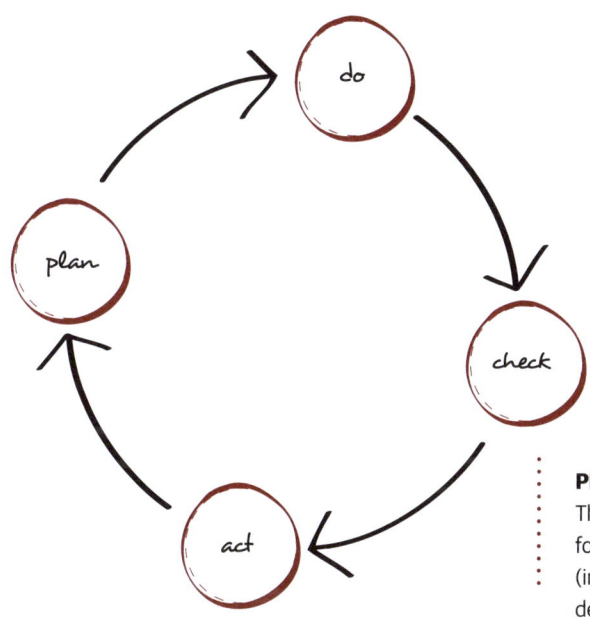

PDCA-model

The same principle forms the basis of the model for quality improvement: Plan – Do – Check – Act (in which 'act' represents adjustment of the action), developed by William Edwards Deming. It is generally regarded as the foundation of good process management and quality management. Repetition of the cycle is the mainstay for eventually producing improvement. And that is a very good fit with Scrum.

/ The reflective practitioner

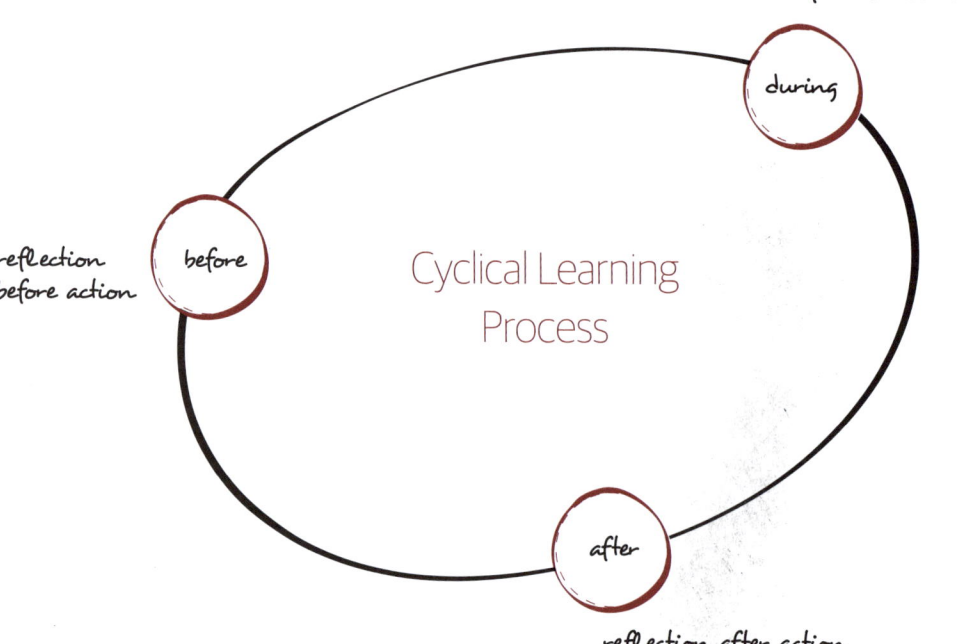

Framework for reflective practice

Back in the 1980s I came in contact with the work of philosopher Donald Schön. He introduced the concept of *The Reflective Practitioner* and wrote a book under that title that is still a bestseller. He has also written a wonderful book about how to train a reflective practitioner (*Educating the reflective practitioner*). Reflection, he says, is a continuing process that takes place not only before and after but also during the action. This way you develop professional knowledge, he asserts.

Professionals are often taught that they ought to use the most firmly proven theories of their discipline in order to become a professional. Schön is opposed to any overly technical application in this respect. He terms that 'technical rationality' and counters it with 'reflection-in-action', whereby the professional may recruit any relevant theories, including the tacit knowledge he himself possesses: a concept that I first encountered with him.

In his book *Frame Reflection*, Schön writes about developing frames and how to play with these in order to create the shape of change. Framing is nothing more than assigning a certain value or meaning to something. The key to frame reflection is learning to think from the perspective of the other or others: what do they find important, and how do they appreciate all the elements of the proposed change?

For me, framing is the core process of communication and thus an important aspect of managing communication. Like the book by Goffman, *Frame Analysis*, this book by Schön is also a 'must read' for communication professionals.

/ Organizational change

'It is not the strongest of the species that survives, nor the most intelligent that survives. It is the one that is the most adaptable.'

Charles Darwin

Planned or Adaptive Change

Finally, I also looked at what organizational theory teaches us. One of the most prominent distinctions is between planned and adaptive change, also called the difference between a design approach and a development approach. In a design approach change is a one-off and linear process with a clear goal and a detailed predetermined plan. The design approach recognizes change as a solution to shortcomings with a clear separation between the planning and the execution of change. Its implementation is permeated with the objective of making the change acceptable in retrospect. The development approach is quite another story. Here it is not the deficiencies or shortcomings, but the concept of advancing knowledge that is the source for the process of change. Members of the organization should be involved in this process, because they know best what the problems are and therefore constitute the best source of information. There is an approximate planning and a lot of room for interim adjustment and there is no detailed pre-designed plan. It will be no surprise that I find the development approach more interesting than the design approach, because the development approach chimes with agile working.

The part played by communication in the change process differs dramatically between the design and the development approaches. Everything in the design approach revolves around the passing on of information about the change and gaining the support of employees, whereas in the development approach communication is the basis of the change process: without communication a change process will never ever fly.

The development approach goes hand in with a vision of communication as an ongoing process of creating meanings, from a transactional, diachronic perception of how communication works.

/ **The power of Scrum**

/ Scrum puts emphasis on quickly delivering the most added value

/ Scrum provides quality, transparency and predictability

/ Scrum stimulates early feedback

/ Scrum ensures that everyone is happy doing what they are good at

/ Scrum is a matter of just going for it: you can start with Scrum immediately

Jeff Sutherland, Rini van Solingen and Eelco Rustenburg in *The Power of Scrum*

/ 10 Steps to start with RCS

1 / Make sure you have a client who endorses Scrum
2 / Formulate a realistic ambition showing what you're aiming for
3 / Find a good Scrum master to safeguard the process
4 / Put an ideal team together and secure the right alliances
5 / Think as early as possible about the potential backlog
6 / Secure adequate mandate from management
7 / Know your stakeholders and keep them on board
8 / Harvest the social stories and take them as a starting point
9 / Establish a nice (eventual digital) Scrum room including a Scrum board
10 / Just start, it's learning by doing

A loose interpretation of Michael Franken's 10 steps in *Scrum voor Dummies*

/ **Biography of Betteke van Ruler**

Dr. Betteke van Ruler is Professor Emerita in Communication Science at the University of Amsterdam, and specializes in corporate communication and public relations. She began her career as a communication professional, moving after 17 years to higher education and then to academic scholarship. She has always been engaged in professional development, of the professional herself and of the concept of corporate communication and public relations as a whole. She is lauded for her ability to bridge the gap between theory and practice and is a sought-after speaker. Students and professionals hang on her every word, not least because they like her ideas and her humor, but because she always couples back to practice. She recently came up with the glossy *Communication NOW*. An English book on Reflective Communication Management is in the making in collaboration with her former colleague Professor dr. Dejan Vercic from Slovenia, as well as an English version of her latest book, *The Strategic Communication Frame*, an agile method for developing a strategy, written with GKSV consultant and former student Frank Körver. She constantly pursues innovation in the discipline of communication, not for the sake of renewal itself, but in the hope that professionalism will improve and that communication management will gain value.

/ **Work in progress**

This presentation of the Reflective Communication Scrum is not definitive. In software terms it's a beta version. It's a matter of learning by doing. In experimenting with the method it will be further refined. So I look forward to your input of many best practices to grasp pitfalls and difficulties, and for you and me to get a hold of the real beauty of the method.

I sincerely hope that you will share your insights and experiences with me on my website at **www.bettekevanruler.nl,** to exchange views, discuss the method and learn how to practice Scrum and other forms of agile working. By doing so we'll work together to keep the method up-to-date in order to meet the challenges of our complicated daily practice. Scrum can help you to be accountable!

/ **Glossary**

- **Accountability** — being responsible to someone for some activity

- **Agile** — flexible, smart, procedurally convenient

- **Coach, coaching** — supervisor, guidance

- **Counseling** — advising at strategic level on compounding the style of the house with society

- **Formative evaluation** — interim evaluation, for example by monitoring

- **Framing** — assigning a specific meaning to a phenomenon

- **Intervention** — deliberate action

- **Social mood** — the village pump as the catalyst of social stories

- **Monitor** — research method for estimating a situation as realistically and reliably as possible

- **Portfolio** — set of interventions to realize an ambition

- **Scrum master** — the linchpin in the RCS who makes the project succeed and the team persevere

- **Scrum** — the method itself and short stand-up meeting in which the team together discuss how to continue

- **Social stories** — conversations showing what people really think about things

- **Sprint** — defined time period in which the team goes to work

- **Summative evaluation** — ex-post evaluation

- **T-shaped person** — content specialist with great ability to work together with other disciplines

- **Outcome** — also known as 'impact'; relates to the difference made, while output relates to what you have done

- **Validation** — at the end of the sprint the client, the team and the Scrum master look back together at results and process

/ **List of references**

Es, Rob van (2012). *De juiste vragen durven stellen (post the right questions)*. In Betteke van Ruler, Communicatie NU (pp. 96-98). Amsterdam, NL: Adfogroep.

Franken, Michael (2013). *Scrum voor Dummies*. Amsterdam, NL: Pearson Benelux.

Hoogendoorn, Sander (2012). *Dit is Agile [This is Agile]*. Amsterdam, NL: Pearson Benelux.

Jongerius, P., Offermans, A., Vanhoucke, A., Sanwikarja P., & Geel, J. van (2013). *Get agile*. Amsterdam, NL: BIS Publishers.

Lewin, Kurt (1946). Action Research and Minority Problems, *Journal of Social Issues 2*(4): 34–46. Retrieved from http://onlinelibrary.wiley.com.

Schön, D.A. (1983). *The Reflective Practitioner: How Professionals Think in Action*. New York, NY: Basic Books.

Schwaber, Ken (2014). *Agile Project Management with Scrum*. Redmond, WA: Microsoft Press.

Schwaber, Ken, & Sutherland, Jeff (2013/1991). *The Scrum Guide*. Retrieved from www.Scrum.org.

Scriven, Michael (1974). Evaluation perspectives and procedures. In W. James Popham (Ed.), *Evaluation in education: Current applications* (pp. 3-94). Berkeley, CA: McCutchan.

Scriven, Michael (1991). Pros and Cons about Goal-Free Evaluation. *American Journal of Evaluation. 12*(1): 55-62.

Shannon, C.E., & Weaver, W. (1949). *The Mathematical Theory of Communication*. Urbana, IL: University of Illinois Press.

Smith, R.D. (2013). *Strategic Planning for Public Relations* (4th ed.). New York and London: Routledge.

Sutherland, Jeff, Van Solingen, Rini, & Rustenburg, Eelco (2011). *The Power of Scrum*. Cambridge, MA: Scruminc.

Takeuchi, H., & Nonaka, I. (1986). The New New Product Development Game. *Harvard Business Review*, 137-146, Jan/Feb. Retrieved from the internet 02.20.2014. https://www.iei.liu.se/fek/frist/723g18/articles_and_papers/1.107457/TakeuchiNonaka1986HBR.pdf

Taleb, Nassim Nicholas (2007). *The Black Swan: The Impact of the Highly Improbable*. New York, NY: Random House.

Luis Gonçalves *Getting Value out of Agile Retrospectives - A Toolbox of Retrospective Exercises*

'Rituals bring people together, allowing them to focus on what is important and to acknowledge significant events or accomplishments.'

/ Notes

/ Notes